KEELING

poems by

Sarah Peecher

Finishing Line Press
Georgetown, Kentucky

KEELING

ACKNOWLEDGMENTS

Immense gratitude to the readers, editors, and staff of the following publications in which these poems previously appeared:

+doc: "Emerging from a silver foil cocoon after the conflagration," nominated for a Pushcart Prize
Agapanthus: an earlier version of "Diplopia: Short Drive."
Allium: A Journal of Poetry & Prose: an earlier version of "Transcription of a Landscape of Memories"
Anti-Heroin Chic: "Marigold, Strawberry Blonde"
Apofenie: an earlier version of "The Girl Plots a Controlled Burn" and "Integrated Loss of Attachment"
The Aurora Journal: "Gallery Talk"
The Bitchin' Kitsch: "Assembly Hall, 2009"
Bluestem: "There are an average of 22 nonfatal drownings per day"
The Lincoln Review: "On Secrets"

The poem "Wayfinding" was selected as the winner of the Allen and Lynn Turner Commencement Poetry Competition 2023.

Publisher: Leah Huete de Maines
Editor: Christen Kincaid
Cover Art: Ryan Lucas
Author Photo: Varya Bazalev
Cover Design: Elizabeth Maines McCleavy

Order online: www.finishinglinepress.com
also available on amazon.com

Author inquiries and mail orders:
Finishing Line Press
PO Box 1626
Georgetown, Kentucky 40324
USA

Contents

Marigold, Strawberry Blonde

Before that first fear, I stood.
A girl at a precipice, a cliff
above an umber, carpeted abyss,
one plush silken body with a plastic face
in each of my fists, blanket trailing
like a gown. Desire for something—
I can't remember what—at the bottom
of the cavern, filled my tiny rose-gold head.
I began my descent
slipped suddenly on the second tread
my body flung like a wilted flower.
Slamming my skull on the cool floor, I
lay silent in the amber dark before
the shock ripped my vocal cords open—
my worry of brokenness soon mirrored
in my parents' wide eyes.

                After my millionth fear,
I just kept walking, clutching the firm glass
of a bottle of malbec.
Feeling cold as a polar vortex wind,
I played it back:
the rush of the white Mustang,
my legs hurrying in slow motion,
my own scream sounding outside of my head.
If it kept playing forward—
the crush, the flare of red and blue lights
against splayed petals of skin.
The voices of my friends reached me
somewhere deep within—*are you okay?*
It felt strange to say yes,
and so quickly.

Assembly Hall, 2009

If I wrote

> *a swaying crowd beneath a parachute*
> *ceiling, lingering scent of popcorn and*
> *pyrotechnics, echoes of funky Jesus*
> *music from towering speaker stacks*

would you feel like you've attended that concert, too, even though
it's a half-sketch of the images from that night?

Maybe there's more to this memory than the concert itself, like the
streams of crowds winding the circumference of the venue, or the hill
of graveled snow I climbed with my friend in the parking lot.

Or her brother, a couple years older than us, in his moto jacket with
layers of pockets, offering his sweaty palm as I descended the hill.

Remembering how that touch felt electromagnetic, warm and particled.

An invisible aurora borealis arcing overhead, slowing time.

Snow wiped from jeans, a torn ticket stub stuffed into my purse,
the clunky van door handle, the texture of polyester, or the proximity
of his long eyelashes and rumpled hair as he pulled the seatbelt
across his body in the seat ahead of me.

And then I'm sitting, studying the nape of his neck, assembling the
shape of his shoulders in glances, my heart bounding like an arctic hare
toward my tingling fingertips, my friend chattering on and on.

Don't cause your classmates to stumble

There wasn't a uniform,
just a paragraph of rules
in the handbook:
Wear polos or shirts with a collar.
Nothing too tight or revealing.
No unnatural hair colors.
Do not draw attention to
the individual.
We reserve the right to
interpret our policies
however we want.

I bought two pairs of pants
two sizes too large
and had them taken in
only at the waist.
I pinned my favorite
thrifted floral top
at the neck
since it dipped past
my collarbone.
I even wore a tank top
tucked in
under every shirt.

I prayed my clothes
wouldn't tattle on me.
Dear God, I wanted
all of my soft skin
my rounding hips
my underwire-branded
ribs to be miraculously,
eternally invisible. I wanted
to be a soul without
a body that could damn
and be damned.

My physics teacher
said I had nicer legs
than the boy who took my seat.
My friends said

I had the curviest hips
out of everyone.
My classmates voted me
best dressed.

An Etymology of "Skinny"

The family doctor studies my spine, watches me walk
the length of the room. Then he raises his rainbow chart

taps his pen on the blue section labeled underweight.
He reassures me that it's fine for my age.

He mumbles something along the lines of *she'll fill out*
as a static-electric worry emanates from my mom.

In the curtained corner, I pull blue-checked fabric over
my goosebump skin which clings close to my bones

while gazing into the hamper, conjuring up images of
girl-bodies fuller than mine filling the gowns stashed there.

I unfurl my clothes, clamber back into their heat
the familiar safety of their neat stack.

My stomach grumbles under my buttoned jeans
empty again though I eat everything, fill it constantly.

When I pull back the curtain, my mom smiles
nods, tells me she looked just like me at my age.

She shows me her thin limbs in a basketball team photo
taken just before a doctor repaired the ruptured disc in her back.

I look at her now, her arms and torso like melted wax
molded in soft layers from when she bore my body, became fuller.

There is a future where I can only see myself clearly in
photos, not mirrors, unfamiliar with my woman-body

where I must remind myself occasionally, not constantly,
I am becoming more whole, more   more.

There is a future where my granny greets me with
you're looking skinny as if it's something desirable

something I have managed to stay.

Transcription of a Landscape of Memories
after the painting Summer *by Joan Snyder*

Entry I

An ensemble of luminous warm tones clusters at the center.
August-dry strokes of saffron crumble at their edges,
spackle into a vivid, vibrating sunset.
The single silver cloud above becomes cumulonimbus.
Brings rain to the pavement where tires screech into meadowed ditch,
cab cracks wooden poll in half, and visor whips into my mom's eye.

Entry II

Opposing blues hang in rectangles
here and there.

Some are small waves   dripping
like my hair   after a dip in the lake.
There seems to be so much   water in summer.
                    Humidity.

The others are sunbaked robin's egg slats
a hue I pick whenever my mom asks
about painting the front door
as we wander the perimeter of our
dewy lawn.

Entry III

Some strokes escape containment—
chartreuse   forest   deep maroon shadow seeping.
          Is the grass getting parched?   Beneath the surface
the lake thickens with dark   but my mom's
bruised eye heals brighter. I bring my boyfriend to the lake
          that summer   my mom warns me

not to wear the turquoise two-piece
                    around my uncle
my swimsuit's bold tint bleeds
          through my striped shirt
                    as we speedboat across the water.

Diplopia: Open Mouths

Thirteen, at the YMCA practicing rebounds
      Twenty-five, walking out the train station exit
launch, bounce, swish, catch, switch sides
      a man in shorts holds open the door behind him
aim for the corner of the red box above the hoop
      does a double-take and opens his mouth
like an angular halo against the clear backboard
      says that he likes my colorful outfit, and I thank him
rhythm interrupted by voices on the half court behind
      I'm wearing a T-shirt with dancing frogs, baggy jeans
a gaze like lasers across the back of my body
      he asks me if I'm an artist, I say yes, I'm a poet
quick on his feet, twirling past his friend for layups
      hope the conversation ends at the bottom of the stairs
quick with his open mouth, to whistle and call
      just to keep the conversation alive, he asks if poets write
just quiet enough I thought I'd imagined it
      what else would a poet do? he thinks they sing
heart hammering, I keep rebounding
      I'm silent, waiting for him to leave.

Body Log

My eardrums remember water pressure.
My cheeks, the clamp of goggle rims. I can still feel
the gentle compression of a navy-blue swim cap
on my forehead, the itch of sun-washed hair strands.
Lungs remember the twinge of nerves
yearning for breath while swimming the full length
of the pool. Thighs remember the tension
of preparing to launch into frigid water.

My chin remembers the prick of a steel sewing pin
in raw pink scars I hide under powder.
Pores still feel the sting of tea tree oil and
suffocate under the tacky clump of makeup.
Browbone remembers the sharp pain
of plucked hair. My lips feel the rasp of teeth
over crusted Carmex skin. The nape of my
neck remembers the sting of the curling iron.

My spine remembers somersaulting to centerstage
in the school's musical production. My lungs remember
the deep breath before launching into a solo,
vocal cords vibrating through time and pitch.
Skin remembers quick changes stage right
and the scrape of tulle and sequins. Waist remembers
the layered compression of pantyhose and corset.
Browbone still feels the glaze of nervous sweat.

My cheek remembers the first soft touch of lips.
My lips still feel the slick of another's spit after
contact with their vermillion and its ridged border.
The walls of my veins and arteries remember
the outward push of blood rushing through.
The nape of my neck, the contour of my waist
still feel the chill of fingertips. My thighs
remember the warm friction of denim.

My knee remembers shooting pain in the middle of
soccer matches, ignored. Shoulder still feels another
taller, stronger body pushing down on it. My forehead
remembers the smack of a ball, ears ringing.
My chest remembers the stream of sweat between
my breasts, pool of wet at the doubled waistband of my shorts.
Drowning in heat, I come up soaked, my lips parched.

Dirty Laundry

I spent hours as a teenager at my too-short oak antique vanity, thighs pressed up against the curved opening with carved flowers, ass aching from the short white stool with painted metal legs and back, though I wouldn't say ass then because to swear was a sin. I did my math or physics homework in pink floral notebooks, frequently fudging the answers by looking them up in the back of the book or asking the internet on my faux-Blackberry cellphone, later a first-generation Apple device. Bored in the middle of a project, I switched to snapping selfies in the wide gold-framed mirror above my makeshift desk, tried to take photos of my long, frizz-curl hair running down my back over my red and blue striped polo, uplit by the two lamps with iridescent brown fabric over their shades, trimmed in delicate pink and brown feathers. For a whole two weeks, when I didn't want to do laundry, I stuffed worn clothes, my favorite pink skort with ditsy flowers, a waffle-knit shirt with sprinting horses printed in crackling blush, underneath my bed with the crinkly bronze-colored patchwork comforter, until my mom found the stash and berated me, asking what I was expecting to accomplish by hiding my dirty laundry.

*

I spent hours   at my   vanity, thighs pressed
up against the   carved flowers,   aching from
white   metal   I wouldn't say
         I did   math   in pink
notebooks, frequently fudging   by
      asking the   faux-Blackberry
           Bored
snapping
     photos of my   hair
        uplit   with iridescent
     shades,   brown feathers
          I stuffed   my
   skort with ditsy flowers,
  crackling blush, underneath my bed   crinkly
        until   mom   berated
        my dirty laundry.

*

I spent hours

in pink

Blackberry

snapping

feathers

underneath

dirty laundry.

On Secrets
a found poem from Mary Ruefle's essay of the same name

Overhearing the world that neither
hides itself
       nor reveals itself,
I listened carefully. I could hear
       singing—

The theory behind intimate conversations
is that we may lose our life.
Samson loses his hair.
Faust loses his soul
       but gains knowledge.

Death and destruction or
self-discovery.
       Curse or incantation.

Folded into notes, the kind you
used to pass in high school,
fragments of the prohibited.
I hid my love because
religious morality is dependent on
       consequence.

I was sunk in a desire to observe
       the stars, to be held.
       Embraced privately.
Just as the astronomer considers
the universe in his mind.

Repressed, then expressed,
I knew exactly what I wanted
and where I wanted it—
a state of reverberation.
       To be changed.
          Unburdened.

I hesitated
       in secret, said nothing.

There are an average of 22 nonfatal drownings per day

Uprooted for the first time, I fend for myself during my seventeenth summer.
That summer, someone bumps the fender of my truck while I'm on lifeguard duty.
Lifeguard drills terrify me; I always struggle to flip the manager over my buoy.
On training nights, we ride our red buoys down the yellow slide at breakneck speeds.
My family visits the chiropractor for whiplash after my dad crashes our truck in the rain.
Dad teaches me how to whip the truck around on snow in the church parking lot.
Driving my brother home from church, the truck skids on ice and we fly into a cornfield.
I take a flight to Peru with a church group to the orphanage my friends used to live in.
Behind the orphanage, my friends and I ride bodyboards down enormous sand dunes.
Dad shows me how to tack boards over the holes in the garden shed to keep out the rain.
As a lifeguard, strapping someone to a backboard is especially hard in a river current.
At swim meets, when the swimmers are at their marks, the whole crowd goes quiet.
In front of the congregation, I fill my lungs before I'm plunged into baptismal water.
I'm not breathing when I'm born and doctors must suck amniotic fluid from my lungs.
Until they cleared my lungs, Mom says it was terribly quiet in that hospital room.

Somewhere near Zaragoza

a woman asks us, *Protestantes o
Católicos?* We don't know exactly
how to respond, so we say,
No me importa. We walk
cobblestone streets through
castled villages, hands stuffed
with pamphlets. Most of the time,
the only sound in each village is
us, a group of Midwestern teens,
tapping our knuckles on doors
and practicing memorized lines
in unison. *Nosotras estamos
en España para dar una biblia
a cada familia que no la tenga.*
Sometimes a dog barks
or a shepherd brings home his flock.
Sometimes a door opens, we recite.
Many people ask if we're
Jehovah's Witnesses. We know
how to tell them we're not
but wonder why they keep asking.
In one of the towns, one of us
accidentally says to a bartender *Te
amo* instead of *Como te llamas?*
At the end of the week, we watch
the Dia de los Reyes Magos parade
while drinking *chocolate
caliente* and eating *rosca
de reyes.* Someone bites into
the baby Jesus hidden in the pastry.
Have we really been doing
the Lord's work?

I'm not sure how to be angry

but I want to write it. I want scream. ugly cry.
I want ugly. I am angry. at something ugly—

the teacher: *comments on underage girl's legs*
them: I'm sure he didn't mean it *like that*

he was taught to be *like that*
        taught to make jokes *like that*
he was taught to be *a man of God* / wdym: he didn't mean it ??

he said something *fucked up* when I dropped his physics class
he didn't pause / feel remorse / apologize

there wasn't anyone who would tell him: *shut the fuck up*
        someone to finally break the rules and curse him
        someone to howl

from across the table at a restaurant
        old friends try to make light of it.
        old friends try to stay bipartisan.
        they say they don't remember any of it—

I try to write it. no one taught me how.
onlytaughtto sit. down. stay calm.

The Girl Plots a Controlled Burn

she slams the back door shut
her heels crush across the fresh lawn

I want

she walks past the shed the garden
to the pile of dried leaves and branches
she squeezes her body into the narrow
space between mud and brush

I want to

it is midafternoon the heat waves
move the prairie grass across the screen
of her vision as she plucks a clover
from the shade nibbles its cool edges

I want to burn

she scrapes a map into the damp earth
marks the swathes of invasive species
and flammable material buildup

I want to burn what hurts

she checks the air for humidity and wind
the conditions must be right or
everything will be destroyed

Wayfinding

feels like
riding a bike
down the gravel road
between fields
full of coneflower
periwinkle, goldenrod
grass, asters. Easy—
though pedaling is hard
teeth chattering
rocks clanking against
the metal bike frame
and it's four miles
to return home.
Laying under a locust tree
surprised by a sudden
dangling inchworm
a sticky memory
sliding down on a brain-string
making shoulders shiver
shake.
Night noises
whispers and creaks
still perceptible under
cellos and piano
buzzing from a boombox.
Standing on hot
asphalt during a
summer storm
refreshed by rain
tingling before lightning
streaks the clouds
and running inside to
wrap up in a beach towel
fresh from the dryer.
Fog
the next morning,
or the things
hidden by it
giants made of mud
entirely imagined,
almost visible.

Integrated Loss of Attachment

White letters on a beat-up black van:
"god entered my body
                    like a body."

Where is god
            in the hollow
the waxy shell of an old man
who isn't there anymore?

In the room of his dying—

I played some memorized sonata
on an old Casio keyboard
halting, stumbling
over the notes on small keys.
My grandfather brought his soft palms
together in applause.

Years later, my husband's
grandmother sings
"How Sweet to Trust in Jesus"
in her crumbling alto.
Her second husband wraps his soft palm
around hers.

Our music twines time.
Our song, exhaust pipe for
soul-fumes
drafting skyward.

god leaves the body—

Sanctuary

As not the room, but the people in it. As the people who only overrun the holiday services. As the moment where everyone shares candlelight & sings "Silent Night." As the body. As the family joke where my mom is the sphincter. As me being vocal cords & hands.

As a warehouse of a room, maybe. As a modern, cream-colored cavern. As an indoor playground in the children's wing. As hide & seek in the dark corridors of the older building before the children's wing is added. As my body squeezed into a closet full of paint cans in the basement.

As a strip mall megastore repurposed where people speak in tongues. As an inflated plastic dome where people on stilts are just part of the worship. As great acoustics for the horn quartet. As an ornate place gradually emptying over decades.

As the forest & the table. As the Sangamon River & fingers wrapped around utensils. As & & & &.

Heirloom

When the chorus starts
and I begin to sing along, Mom mentions that
her mother never allowed her to listen
to "Karma Chameleon"
because Boy George wore makeup.

We pull up to the house as
the car becomes a confessional:

Mom watched an explicit '80s movie as a preteen
her mother would have despised
if she had found out about it.

> When I ask about it to gauge how bad
> it might have been
> she doesn't remember
> which movie it was

Mom cuts the engine, opens the door
but doesn't get out. We sit in semi-stagnant
heat while she digs in the console for
a McAlister's napkin to use as a tissue.

> I know when she pauses like this
> there's more she wants to say
>
> I imagine her taking out
> another memory
> an heirloom piece
> I'm not sure I want to inherit
> frangible and velveteen

She says,
when she was sixteen,
her mother threatened to kick her out of the house
if she didn't find a job that day.

> I will forget about this for months,
> my memory of our conversation
> seeping wordlessly from one ear
> as I spend a night in my creaky childhood bed
> in my parents' new house

When she brought it up last week, she says,
her mother hesitated, at first, to apologize.

Diplopia: Short Drives

The day of the truck crash, someone drove me to church
A few days before the new year, I saw a fox
in my arms the teddy bear the firefighters gave me
carrying a rabbit in its mouth as it crossed the asphalt
it had been raining, which is why we hydroplaned
your dad's headlights caught its dusty terracotta fur
a word I learned later, as my dad diagrammed the accident
it felt like an omen—what does a fox with a rabbit mean?
the sun was shining as I entered the hall of the church
I thought it might mean we'd eat well this year
every day after that, whenever I rode in the car
though it reminded me how, once, a rabbit got stuck
I hyperfocused on the tilt of the fuzzy backseat under me
in the fence of our garden and strangled there
I often gripped the notch in the door or my seatbelt
I saw it the next morning, tried not to look too closely
as the car lurched on the country roads near home
though I had become used to the small dead things
and there's a hazy memory where I told my mom
my cats hunted, then scattered across the back deck
to drive safely, and she told me to calm down.

Previously Unrecorded Portions of Our Vacation

Entry I

The five of us
you, your family, and I
will slide through
the door to cold air, sparkling clean.

We will gasp at the picture window
explore the cupboards
            pick our rooms.
            You and I will make plans for
your midnight escapade
down the
            plush carpeted stairs
                    to my bed.

The lake will be stormy, though it's August.
We will dare
the loser of the card game
            to jump into the
                    rain-drop-rippled pool.
I will not lose, and I won't remember who did.

Entry II

In the morning we will
            descend
                    the grainy, gray stairs
through the pale, spiky stalks of beach grass
the jointed stems of which, broken at various nodes,
poke the soles of our feet,
            to the water's edge. It will be
barely blue
            and icy cold.
In the evening, when the sand is
            warm underfoot, we'll ramble
                    down a mile to the public beach.

Entry III

I study the seagulls.
            Their gray water–repellence.
I've heard it's the same film as a succulent.

Meanwhile, you get a smile and a nod from another man
about my body.
You tell me.
I wonder
if I should feel complimented as I

crunch through
collections of shells, uncomfortable

                                    not in pain.

I smile in the video you record of me
            leaping down from the rocks
in my second ever two-piece swimsuit

and off-camera
I'm preoccupied with wondering
whether secretly sleeping with you
is really a sin,
            sand lodging itself between
            my diary entries.

Green Thumb

"I'm not sure how to begin that poem," I say
as we each take a sip of our iced lattes.
She asks me if I share any experiences with
that queer poet I love—if I could emulate him, maybe.

A bee interrupts our conversation,
hovering back and forth above our drinks
landing on a marigold in a nearby planter
reminding me of the seeds I planted
in my mom's garden a few days earlier.

I say, "I can't,
because I didn't start coming out until my twenties.
I've only ever come out to supportive friends.
I'm married to a man."

I think, *no one has ever called me slurs*
and I haven't told my mom that I'm bisexual.
That poet's experienced a lifetime of hurt
that I've simply avoided.

I read how his mom reacted when he came out.
Slapped him across the face. She told him
never to tell his brothers.

The last time my mom was in Chicago
she spilled tears over our lattes. As usual,
I wanted to crank the spigot closed,
tried to mason-jar my annoyance.

My response to her tears grew in
strange angles during my girlhood.
While she sniffled at church every week,
my body and mind stiffened to this
evolutionary adaptation meant to soften.

She'd learned her horticultural techniques
in fragments from her mother,
then turned to the Almanac,
followed its instruction on
how to carve out what's natural,

provide structure to the looseness of plant life,
leave no room for fluorescent pests.

There's a winding string that ties
my mom's ability to garden the hell out of a backyard
to the worry I'll suddenly stick like a thorn in her palm
and the surprise in her eyes will
make her want to suddenly yank.

Trying to express how the risk of her tears
has kept me hushed, lush in foliaged silence,
I turned on the tap of her tears.

I extended my hand across the white marble table
to offer her a crinkled napkin for her teary face.
She set down her latte to take it.

Burned Album

It started with "Rumour Has It" above the din of a watered-down suburban franchise restaurant, Dad purchased Adele's album on iTunes, burned the album to a CD and scrawled the title and artist in his loose, flowing handwriting on its rainbow-mirrored surface, gave it to me one day in the car, I spent hours with those mournful ballads. I transitioned to curated playlists of bright, jangly indie pop interspersed with ad breaks, to a Pop and Hip Hop Power Workout playlist at the YMCA, my mom was furious about anything explicit, pop music in Dad's Dodge Dakota driving my brother and I to school. I spent a whole snow day listening to *Dialects*, the greyscale cover art a photograph of two people from far out, one on the edge of a cliff, one hovering in midair over the canyon, distant and dream-like, one review said cinematic. I listen to the album again, flutes, strings, thrumming drumbeats, that snowy afternoon in February I spent planning a Pinterest life, sometimes I wish I could hear it with new ears, I want that magic again, that lock opening internally, a piece of myself I didn't know was missing sliding back into place.

*

It started with   the din of a
                                                                    burned
        album   loose, flowing
                                                            one day in the
car, I   transitioned to
                    jangly   Pop
            Power   mom   furious about
anything explicit   in Dad's Dodge   driving
                                                    to *Dialects*,
                                                        on the edge of
            midair
        I listen to the   thrumming

                with new ears   that lock
                                                    sliding back

*

It started with   a

Dialect
　　on the edge of

　　thrumming

　　　　　lock
　　sliding back

Gallery Talk

Every morning the yesterday girl becomes more yesterday.

Every morning the today woman is more today, this hour, now.

The woman asks, "Where are you going yesterday girl?"

I'm tucking myself into the back corner of your brain.

In the lamp-lit back corner, the yesterday girl crawls into the blanket fort built there.

The today woman drinks a lavender oat milk latte at her desk, taps her long fingernails on her keyboard without typing anything.

The woman maps her way to the back corner to offer the girl a sip.

The girl says, *No thank you, I don't like coffee.*

"But it's sweet. It tastes like a delicious bath."

The girl doesn't take baths anymore, she showers, though she loves to take her time, put too much soap on the washcloth and squeeze the suds out.

"Do you remember getting in trouble for using mom's razor as a squeegee in the shower?"

I don't want to talk about that. I hate getting in trouble. The girl's face reddens.

The today girl wonders if the woman spotted her face in the crowd yesterday.

In her dreams, the woman is yesterday again, trying to conceal her naked body behind a locust tree in the backyard.

The today girl, when she's lying awake at night, wonders if anyone actually likes her jokes.

The girlwoman dresses up as a marigold fairy.

The todayyesterdaywomangirl will be a mythical creature for just a little bit longer.

Scarlet Bar, 2022

At the gay bar
no one danced
with me.

I danced
with everyone.

We sang every song
making eye contact
while we crooned
with no expectation
of further connection.

The room heated
with movement, spun
with strings of light.

A super-
organism
of pulsing
hyperpop.

I wasn't there
alone, invited
unbeknownst
as a third wheel.

I didn't care—
at Scarlet they play
the best music.

Charli's voice
perforated
the pink cloud
of a woman's perfume.

My husband
was at home.
I wondered what
it would be like
just to kiss

that woman's
perfume.

There was an expiration
time, the end of
the DJ's set
at 11:00 p.m.

What if I
met a woman
like the ones
in my dreams?

I looked toward
my friend
and his date.
He was
kissing him.

At the end of the night
we reeled toward home
rambling about
who knew which songs
best.

For knowing half
of Charli's discography
my friend's date said
I could have an honorary
F** Hag Card.
I pictured a holographic
card with someone
purply, witchily gay
on it.
My leather-jacketed
friend said
No...   —no!
as I unknowingly
agreed.

Laughable
after I found out
the next morning
a woman like that
is almost always
straight and
very strange.
Wished I hadn't
felt too sick
from one too many
Sapphire gin
and tonics
to say

No...   —no!
You've got
me wrong.

The Girl Surveys the Firebreak

she places her camcorder in a tree
  to track the fire's progress while
    she wades the boundary of the burning—
      a cool creek that splashes ash clean from her calves
        her left shoulder, exposed thighs below green cargo shorts
          prickle warm as though recently sunburned

            she pauses
          studies the low, vibrant
              orange and yellow blooms
            billowing into opalescent plumes
              phantom coreopsis, bluestem
                their burial beneath embers
                  signals imminent flourishing

                  she reaches the road
                      plants herself on the concrete slope
                          beneath the bridge
                        listens to a tractor thunder overhead
                      determines her timelapse
                          must have enough footage by now

                    later she conducts a solo viewing on the
                  TV in her rusty-metal-doored closet
                    on the staticky screen
                the blaze leans back
                      then forward as the air
                  breathes into it—
                its fingers
              rapidly float and flex
          as they grab up the slender dead
        carry them to the sky
      this is what keeps the prairie a prairie, she thinks,
    bowing her head toward the orange glow,
  if you take this out, everything changes.

A Lesson

She took a paper packet
of seeds in her fingers,

smudged with the deep brown
of loam, and tore it,

poured the dormant wisps
into her smooth open palm.

She prodded them, last year's
remnants dried in the basement,

charcoal fragments with honey
feathers. We'd excavated

the garden bed in long, shallow
lines, relocating earthworms

to new sites. Mom was not
unsettled by the sleeping grubs

while I stabbed at them with
the tines of my cultivator.

She scattered the seeds
and told me feelings are

neither right nor wrong.
We tucked them into the soil.

Emerging from a silver foil cocoon after the conflagration

I'm wearing my lime green pants with huge pockets & my hair is in bubble braids. You will not catch me in your butterfly net. I've got my stompiest boots on. I am the wild fourth season of *Search Party*. After all the smoke & mirrors, I will finally be honest—I don't want to be modest. I am a medley & melodious & I will look the part.

*

What is this handbloom?
Peony of singed pages
destroying-making.

*

I'll adorn you in Joseph's technicolor coat
when the wind blesses us with frigid kisses.
Spicy shrimp chips crunch their way through your teeth.
What exactly do you divine from crumbs of burnt incense?

I excavate the patio, plant wildflowers instead.
Where will we go when the air is too dry to breathe?
We sit in the coffee shop; you hum along to pop punk.
You've inherited a throat-clearing habit & I tell myself it's cute.

Every once in a while, some memory from the past jolts me.
I'm keeling in my platform boots, but don't worry, I refuse to twist an ankle.
You lumber out of your clothes & dance toward the closet.
I negotiate the sidewalk, making eye contact with dogs & not their owners.

I've tried to outmaneuver slick roads, but I couldn't manage it.
The cat practices bird sounds, cackling like the little flame she is.
Freshly out of the shower, you quake until I bring you a towel.
My favorite blanket, thin & soft blue, rests on the end of the bed.

I try to count the tiny pink buds on the trees, but there are so, so many.
By underpin me, I mean hold me while I avoid sleep demons.
I'll whittle it down until it makes sense.
I'll xerox you a stink bug, even though I've never done it before.
I'll be your Wizzrobe, floating, prancing, zapping.

*

There are several moments
of heavy, blanket silence
like

[   ]

[   ]

[   ]

rooted in some
fragment of feeling.
I want to crawl under them
& remember.

                                        *

I crack open my front window
to tell the budding maple tree
my name means *princess*
& it makes me cringe
though maybe it shouldn't.

I'm named after a woman
who laughed at God.
She was a loyal nomad
& a doubtress.

I'm getting distracted by
the scraggly squirrel napping
on one of the maple's branches.

This Biblical woman, she was so hot
that a pharaoh wanted her.
Her husband pretended to
be her brother, which was a half-lie,
so he wouldn't wind up dead.
Don't get me started on the situation
with Hagar. The first Sarah was a
complicated woman &
the mother of a nation. I might be

complicated, but I'm not sure
I want children. I think,
like my mom has often said,
I'm selfish.

I tell my dear, pink-tipped tree a secret:
I've always been The Responsible One
& I don't want to be anymore.

I want to be like you, whooshing
as winter winds disco your branches.
Holding out limbs to scraggly creatures.
Breathless & thriving in summer heat.

*

The epiphany is never &
                forever
lurking in the corner
while the party guests spiral
& serenade one another about life's
meaninglessness &
       fullness

NOTES

"Assembly Hall, 2009" is after John Keene's poem, "Herring Cove Beach, 1997," and "The Curator Plots a Controlled Burn" is after his poem, "The Art Theater, 1986."

"Scarlet Bar, 2022" dances to the beat of Sandra Cisneros' poem "Tea Dance, Provincetown, 1982," especially the borrowed first two stanzas.

"The Curator Wanders the Firebreak" owes much of its existence to the University of Montana's podcast *Fireline*. It also adapts a quote from Bill Sproul in *National Geographic*'s article "The Great Plains prairie needs fire to survive. These ranchers are bringing it back."

"A Lesson" is after Ada Limón's poem "The First Lesson."

"Emerging from the silver foil cocoon after the conflagration": This poem was crafted in response to prompts from "You Must Use the Word Smoothie: A Craft Essay in 50 Writing Prompts" by Chen Chen.

WITH THANKS

To Tony Trigilio for helping me bring this body of work to life. I appreciate your gentle guidance, contagious excitement about our precious field of work, and our conversations about cats.

To C.M. Burroughs for teaching me to obsess diligently, to include the body wherever possible, and to notice when I "put my foot in it." Thank you for sharing your story with me and inspiring in me the courage to share my own.

More gratitude and big bouquets of wildflowers to: David Trinidad, Madeline McConico, Annalise Nassani, Kala Wahl, Bea Forkan, DeAndre Holmes, Amelia Dellos, Jay Bigboy, Emoonah McClerklin, Erin Hattamer, Michelle Alexander, Ankita Sadarjoshi, Spencer Washington, Lor Clincy, Erica McKeehen, Siera Carpenter, Andrew Warrick, and Marc Meiercort.

Gratitude to my dear friends, Rachel and Em, who send me memes and commiserate about our shared Evangelical upbringings. You create space for me to talk, be angry, and laugh about these things. You deserve all the love and joy life brings you.

Deepest gratitude to my love, Elijah. This simply would not be possible without you. It's a delight to be thriving with you, today.

www.ingramcontent.com/pod-product-compliance
Lightning Source LLC
Chambersburg PA
CBHW020220090426
42734CB00008B/1153